WE
THE PEOPLE
PONTIAC

Library of Congress Cataloging-in-Publication Data

Rothaus, James.
  Pontiac.

  (We the people)
  Summary: Examines the life of the Ottawa warrior
who became a great war chief and united his people
against the encroachment of the British in the eighteenth
century.
  1. Pontiac, Ottawa Chief, d. 1769—Juvenile literature.
2. Ottawa Indians—Biography—Juvenile literature.
[1. Pontiac, Ottawa Chief, d. 1769.   2. Ottawa Indians—
Biography.   3. Indians of North America—Biography]
I. Title.   II. Series: We the people (Mankato, Minn.)
E83.76.P66R68   1987   973.2'7'0924   [B] [92]   87-27180
ISBN 0-88682-160-6

WE
THE PEOPLE
PONTIAC

INDIAN GENERAL AND STATESMAN
(1720-1769)

JAMES R. ROTHAUS

Illustrated By Harold Henriksen

CREATIVE EDUCATION

PONTIAC

Early explorers couldn't believe their eyes. They returned to Europe with exciting stories of five vast lakes that stretched for hundreds of miles through the northern woodlands of the New World. They called them the Inland Seas of America. Today, we know them as the Great Lakes—Superior, Michigan, Huron, Erie and Ontario.

The first white men to live around the Great Lakes were French fur traders and missionaries. They found three large Indian tribes there— the Chippewa, the Potawatomi, and the Ottawa. All were allies.

Of the three tribes, the Ottawa were least friendly to the whites. They refused to become Christians, and they remained suspicious of the strangers.

Still, the Ottawa liked the French trade goods. They traded furs for guns, cloth, knives, needles, pots, and rum. Soon, they forgot their old way of life and came to depend on the things they obtained from the trading posts. They built their villages nearby.

About 1720, a boy named Pontiac was born in an unknown Ottawa village. Later he seems to have lived in a village near Fort Detroit. His home was a hut called a wigwam, made of poles covered with bark.

Each spring, hundreds of Indians visited the fort and traded. The French were kind to them and there was peace among the tribes of the Great Lakes.

Young Pontiac grew tall and

strong. Of all the young Ottawas, he was the best at telling stories around the fire. His imagination was keen and rich. Even the elders were amazed by the way Pontiac could paint pictures in their minds with his words.

When he was about 16, Pontiac became a warrior. Each summer, the Ottawas and their allies went to war. They fought the Shawnees and Iroquois. These tribes had been moving westward as British settlers crowded them out of their old lands.

Soon, Pontiac became a famous war chief. Besides being brave, he used his way with words to unite all warriors behind him. Inspired by his speeches, even Pon-

tiac's rivals soon fell under his spell.

In 1754, the French and British went to war to decide which would control the lands shown on the map. The Ottawa and other western tribes fought on the side of the French. Their customary way of making war was very cruel. The warriors killed not only soldiers, but also unarmed settlers, women, and children.

The British came to hate and fear all Indians—even friendly ones.

The French and Indian War ended in 1760. The French lost. They had to move out of their forts and give up trading with the Indians. The British hurried to send their own soldiers to these forts.

Pontiac sent warriors to the edge of the forest. He told them to watch the British. "Tell me the names of the white chiefs," he commanded. "Count the soldiers in each fort. Count the muskets and the cannons, too. See if the white soldiers are lazy or drunk. Then we shall see our next step."

Unlike the French, the Brit-

13

ish troops were very disciplined and organized. They were clever, too. They sent smooth-talking officers to make friends with the Indians. At first, the British promised Pontiac's people that everything would be better than before. But soon things were worse. British traders cheated the Indians. Settlers began to take Indian lands. The whites no longer gave them rum and gunpowder for their furs.

Two years passed. Pontiac grew more and more angry at what he felt were wrongs done to his people by the British. He began to plot. Night after night, he sat with a stick by the fire, scratching war plans in the soft earth. His imagination soared.

Finally, Pontiac's plan was complete. It was truly amazing! For the first time in history, he convinced all the tribes to forget their old quarrels and join together. Once again, Pontiac painted exciting pictures with his words. Only if the red men fought united as one, he said, could they hope to defeat the British.

His plan was later called Pontiac's Conspiracy. He wanted the Indians to attack all the British forts at one time. A war belt of red wampum was sent from Lake Ontario to the Mississippi River. The belt was the symbol of united Indian action.

On May 7, 1763, Chief Pontiac signalled the start of his war against the British. To demonstrate

his own courage, the chief himself led a large band of men into Fort Detroit. They had hidden guns. But someone had warned the British. The Indians had to retreat.

Pontiac was furious. He could not take the fort by surprise, so he attacked the British settlers outside. Then his army surrounded Fort Detroit and lay siege to it.

Pontiac did not harm the French people who still lived nearby. He told them: "We will drive the British away. Then we will give the fort back to you. It will be as it was before, in the good days."

Fort Detroit held fast. So Pontiac sent out bands to attack the other forts. Fort Sandusky fell to the Hurons. Men from Pontiac's own army took Fort Saint Joseph, Fort Miamis, and Fort Ouiatenon.

Far to the north, a band of Chippewas entered Fort Michilimackinac. They pretended to play a game of lacrosse. Then suddenly they attacked the soldiers and took the fort.

Pontiac's plan was working! Never before had the red men enjoyed so much success in war against the whites. Even the tribes which had doubted Pontiac now rushed to join forces to share in the glory.

The British had only one western fort left—Fort Edward Augustus, at Green Bay. There were no troops to help them in case of attack, so the men there were ordered to surrender. They gave

themselves up to friendly Indians.
Now the eastern tribes began
to arise. Delawares attacked farms
around Fort Pitt. Many people were
killed. Others fled to the fort.

Senecas of the Iroquois Nation burned Fort Venango. They chased a small British force out of Fort LeBoeuf. Then an army of Senecas and Ottawas took Fort Presque Isle.

The war was only six weeks old, yet the Indians had already seized nine forts. Two others, Detroit and Pitt, were in grave danger. The

British could hardly believe Pontiac had done it. The news spread throughout England. Could it be? The proud empire's top troops were being wiped out by swarms of Indians led by a demon chief named Pontiac!

Meanwhile, Pontiac himself tried in vain to take Fort Detroit. Two British ships sailed swiftly up the Detroit River to bombard Pontiac's camp with cannon shot. He sent fire rafts against them, but the ships escaped.

Then fresh British troops arrived. Pontiac led a bloody battle that defeated them—but Fort Detroit itself still held. Pontiac hoped that the French would send help. He waited in vain.

The tide of war began to turn when fresh British relief troops finally came to the people holding out at Fort Pitt. The Indians there had to retreat in August. But Pon-

tiac still had Fort Detroit at bay and waited for the French to join him.

Late in October, a French officer brought a letter to Pontiac. The French and British had signed the Treaty of Paris and made peace.

Pontiac had no choice but to give up. Many of his Indian allies were tired of fighting. Winter was coming. They decided to go back to their families. Even Pontiac's fiery speeches couldn't change their minds.

The British tried to capture Pontiac. But he went to Illinois, to talk to the French.

The great conspiracy was over. Pontiac tried to stir up the Illinois Indians against the British, but news of his failure followed him from the East. The French commander at Fort de Chartres refused to help him. The fort was occupied by the British in 1765. Pontiac's vision of a united Indian nation had withered and died. He admitted defeat at last and even helped the British subdue the last scattered bands of Indian fighters.

The great war chief was now a lonely exile in Illinois. Indians who had once followed him now

hated him for giving up. In 1769, the Peoria tribe sent a lone brave to kill him. Pontiac died of a stab in the back in Cahokia, Illinois. But the vision he had scratched in the

earth by the fire ignited a hatred between white men and red that would burn for more than 100 years—until the last western Indian surrendered to the white invaders.

WE THE PEOPLE SERIES

WOMEN OF AMERICA

CLARA BARTON
JANE ADDAMS
ELIZABETH BLACKWELL
HARRIET TUBMAN
SUSAN B. ANTHONY
DOLLEY MADISON

INDIANS OF AMERICA

GERONIMO
CRAZY HORSE
CHIEF JOSEPH
PONTIAC
SQUANTO
OSCEOLA

FRONTIERSMEN OF AMERICA

DANIEL BOONE
BUFFALO BILL
JIM BRIDGER
FRANCIS MARION
DAVY CROCKETT
KIT CARSON

WAR HEROES OF AMERICA

JOHN PAUL JONES
PAUL REVERE
ROBERT E. LEE
ULYSSES S. GRANT
SAM HOUSTON
LAFAYETTE

EXPLORERS OF AMERICA

COLUMBUS
LEIF ERICSON
DeSOTO
LEWIS AND CLARK
CHAMPLAIN
CORONADO